100

things you should know about

VICTORIAN BRITAIN

100

things you should know about

VICTORIAN
BRITAIN

Jeremy Smith

Consultant: Fiona Macdonald

Miles
Kelly

PUBLISHING

First published in 2006 by Miles Kelly Publishing Ltd
Bardfield Centre, Great Bardfield, Essex, CM7 4SL

Copyright © Miles Kelly Publishing Ltd 2006

2 4 6 8 10 9 7 5 3 1

This title also appears in hardback

Publishing Director: Anne Marshall
Editor: Belinda Gallagher
Editorial Assistant: Lisa Clayden
Designer: Michelle Cannatella
Picture Researcher: Liberty Newton
Proofreader: Margaret Berrill
Indexer: Jane Parker

ISBN 1-84236-653-X

Printed in China

British Library Cataloguing-in-Publication Data
A catalogue record for this book is available from the British Library

ACKNOWLEDGEMENTS

The publishers would like to thank the following artists
who have contributed to this book:
Steve Caldwell, Peter Dennis, Mike Foster, Peter Gregory
Sally Holmes, Richard Hook, John James, Janos Marffy,
Alessandro Menchi, Andrea Morandi, Mike Saunders
Graham Sumner, Mike White
Cartoons by Mark Davis at Mackerel

The publishers would like to thank the following sources
for the use of their photographs:
Page 6 (FP) Hulton Deutsch Collection/CORBIS;
20 (M) Columbia/Pictorial Press; 24 (M) Pictorial Press;
25 (ML) Hulton Deutsch Collection/CORBIS;
29 (TR) Historical Picture Archives/CORBIS, (BL) Pictorial Press;
30 (MR) Paramount/Pictorial Press; 31 (MR) Rank/Pictorial Press;
38 (TR) The Salvation Army International Heritage Centre;
(BL) Pictorial Press; 42 (BM) Fotoware a.s 1997-2003; 44 (BM) The Art
Archive/Eileen Tweedy; 46 (FP) Pictorial Press; 47 (ML) Pictorial Press

All other images are from MKP Archives, Dover, ILN, PhotoDisc

www.mileskelly.net
info@mileskelly.net

Contents

The Victorian world

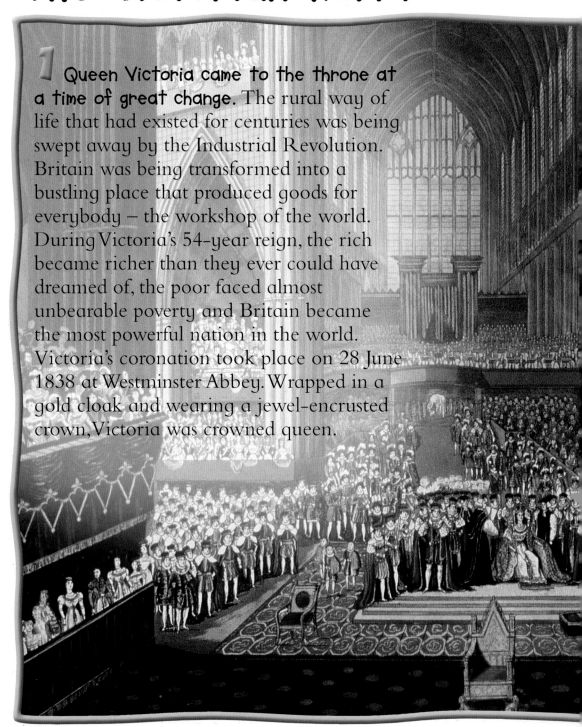

1 **Queen Victoria came to the throne at a time of great change.** The rural way of life that had existed for centuries was being swept away by the Industrial Revolution. Britain was being transformed into a bustling place that produced goods for everybody – the workshop of the world. During Victoria's 54-year reign, the rich became richer than they ever could have dreamed of, the poor faced almost unbearable poverty and Britain became the most powerful nation in the world. Victoria's coronation took place on 28 June 1838 at Westminster Abbey. Wrapped in a gold cloak and wearing a jewel-encrusted crown, Victoria was crowned queen.

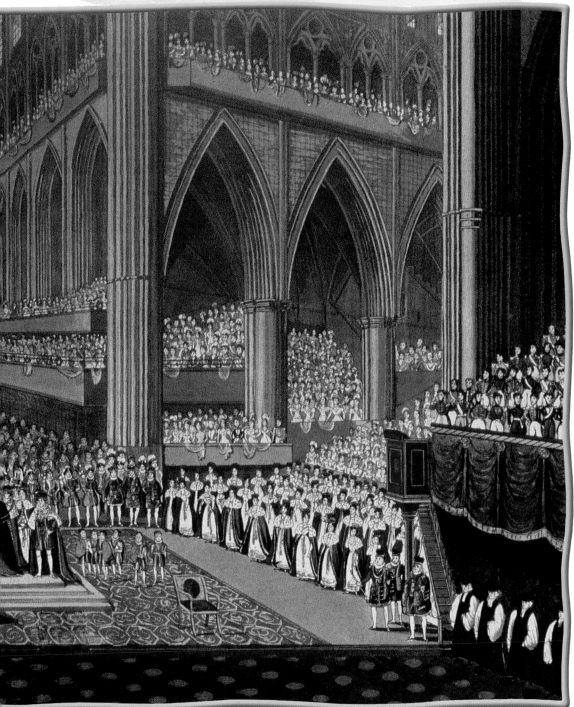

Meet the royals

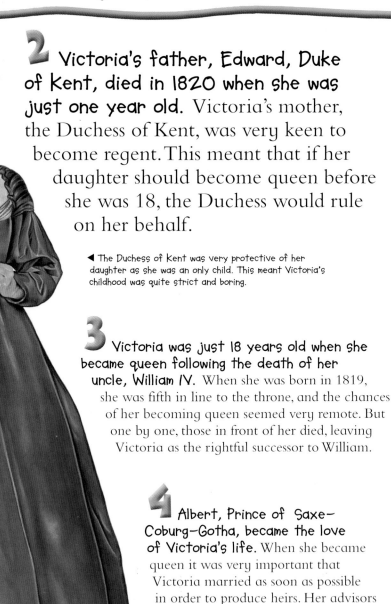

2 **Victoria's father, Edward, Duke of Kent, died in 1820 when she was just one year old.** Victoria's mother, the Duchess of Kent, was very keen to become regent. This meant that if her daughter should become queen before she was 18, the Duchess would rule on her behalf.

◀ The Duchess of Kent was very protective of her daughter as she was an only child. This meant Victoria's childhood was quite strict and boring.

3 **Victoria was just 18 years old when she became queen following the death of her uncle, William IV.** When she was born in 1819, she was fifth in line to the throne, and the chances of her becoming queen seemed very remote. But one by one, those in front of her died, leaving Victoria as the rightful successor to William.

4 **Albert, Prince of Saxe–Coburg–Gotha, became the love of Victoria's life.** When she became queen it was very important that Victoria married as soon as possible in order to produce heirs. Her advisors arranged for her to meet Albert, her handsome German cousin, and the couple fell deeply in love. They married in 1840 in a glittering ceremony at St James's Palace, London.

5 Victoria and Albert had a happy marriage and had nine children together – five daughters and four sons. Their names were Vicky, Edward, Alice, Alfred, Helena, Louise, Arthur, Leopold and Beatrice. Some historians say that the queen was a stern mother, but others say she was warm and loving. Victoria was close to her first daughter, Vicky, but she had an uneasy relationship with her son, Edward.

I DON'T BELIEVE IT!

British law said that no man was allowed to propose to the queen, so Victoria had to ask for Albert's hand in marriage!

6 When Prince Albert died of typhoid at the age of 42, a Scottish gillie (servant) named John Brown became Victoria's most trusted friend. He befriended the queen during her period of mourning and even saved Victoria from an assassination attempt. Many people were suspicious of this close relationship, nicknaming the queen 'Mrs Brown'. When Victoria died, she was buried holding a photograph of her favourite servant.

▼ Like most families in the Victorian era, Victoria and Albert had many children. They valued family life and spent as much time as possible with their children. Sadly, three of Victoria's children died before she did – Alice, Leopold and Alfred.

The greatest Empire

7 **The original founder of the British Empire was Queen Elizabeth I.** She sent a series of explorers, including Sir Francis Drake, around the world to claim new lands for her kingdom. The Empire started life as a handful of colonies along the eastern coast of North America, but by the 1800s it had grown to include India, South Africa and Canada.

English spoken as a first language

English used in government

English spoken among traders

◀ With the Empire at its height, English became the main spoken language of the British Isles, North America, the Caribbean and Oceania. English also became the language of government throughout much of Asia and Africa and was widely used by traders in non English–speaking areas.

8 **During Victoria's reign, the British Empire expanded until it covered one-quarter of the world's surface.** It also included all of the world's main trading routes, making Britain an extremely rich country. Victoria was proud of the British Empire, referring to it as the 'family of nations'.

9 **India was the jewel of the British Empire.** Elizabethan explorers arrived there in the 1500s, but for hundreds of years afterwards the country was ruled not by the queen, but by the British East India Company. In 1858 control passed to the British government after an uprising, and in 1877 Victoria became Empress of India in a lavish ceremony.

10 Many poorer people were desperate to escape poverty in Britain. Some made a fresh start by moving to a different part of the empire, emigrating as far as Australia and New Zealand. Others sought their fortune in the 'New World' of America, which called itself the land of opportunity and the land of the free.

12 Not every country in the empire was happy about being ruled by Britain. British soldiers were sent to all four corners of the empire to make sure countries obeyed Queen Victoria's laws. Towards the end of Victoria's rule, there were actually more British soldiers in larger countries such as India than there were back home.

▼ The Victorians in India practiced British customs such as drinking tea. Many Indians also adopted these customs.

QUIZ

1. Who was the original founder of the British Empire?

2. When did Queen Victoria become Empress of India?

3. Which British sport became popular in India?

4. Which British custom became widely practiced in India?

Answers:
1. Queen Elizabeth I 2. 1877 3. Cricket 4. Drinking tea

11 The British exported their way of life and customs to the countries in the empire. However, local people were allowed to follow their own customs as long as they didn't conflict with British law. New British-style buildings sprang up, and some local people spoke English as their first language. The colonies had their influence on Britain, too. Colonial fashion, such as the wearing of pyjamas, made their way back to Britain during Victoria's reign.

▼ Cricket became popular in India during Victoria's reign and is the number one sport there today.

Britain versus the world

13 The Crimean War with Russia (1853–1856) was very damaging for Britain. Although Britain and her allies won the war, they lost many soldiers during the conflict. The poet Tennyson wrote the poem 'The Charge of the Light Brigade' to remember a disastrous part of the campaign, when thousands of British troops rushed straight into enemy fire. In total, the war cost the lives of 22,000 British soldiers.

14 The Indian Mutiny of 1857 started because of a row over rifle bullets. Indian soldiers heard that animal fat used to grease the cartridges came from cows – animals sacred to Muslims and Hindus. This sparked a rebellion and thousands of soldiers were killed in riots before the revolt was eventually defeated.

◀ Despite suffering terrible early losses during the Mutiny, British troops quickly regained control of India and slaughtered thousands of rebels in revenge.

◄ The Battle of Balaclava took place on 25 October 1854. More than 600 British soldiers charged into enemy fire and almost 250 of them were killed or wounded.

16 During Victoria's reign Britain built a formidable fleet of ships to protect her Empire. By the end of the 19th century, however, the power of the Royal Navy was being threatened by a new fleet of German ships. To prevent the Germans becoming too powerful, a new rule called the two-power standard was brought in. It stated that the Royal Navy must be twice as large as its nearest rival.

15 In 1877, the British seized the South African state of Transvaal from European settlers called Boers. The Boers rebelled and defeated the queen's forces, who were easy targets in their bright red uniforms. Then in 1899 British troops tried to take control of South Africa again after gold was discovered there. This time a mighty British army crushed the Boers and Transvaal and the Orange Free State became British colonies.

▼ HMS *Inflexible* was a mighty iron battleship commissioned by the Royal Navy in 1876. She had the thickest armour of any battleship of her time.

Town and country

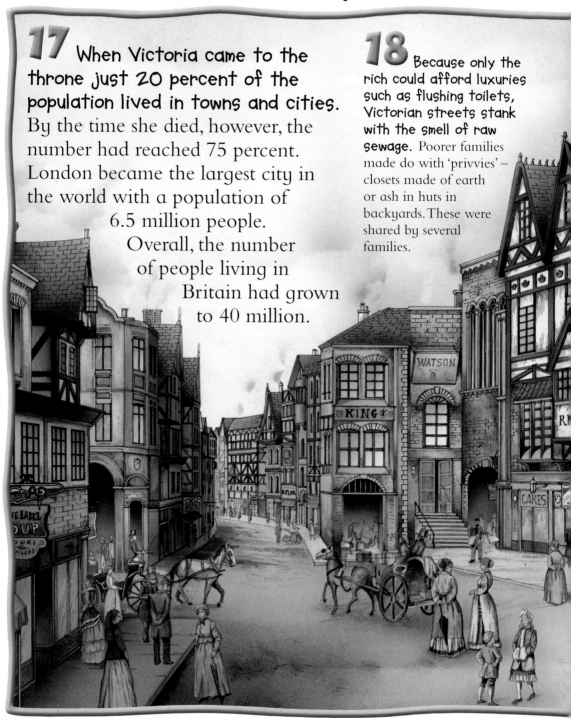

17 When Victoria came to the throne just 20 percent of the population lived in towns and cities. By the time she died, however, the number had reached 75 percent. London became the largest city in the world with a population of 6.5 million people. Overall, the number of people living in Britain had grown to 40 million.

18 Because only the rich could afford luxuries such as flushing toilets, Victorian streets stank with the smell of raw sewage. Poorer families made do with 'privvies' – closets made of earth or ash in huts in backyards. These were shared by several families.

19 The Victorian poor often scratched a living by selling their wares on street corners. People also sold fruit and vegetables on market stalls, or traded bread, milk and pies from hand carts. There were also shoe-shiners who polished people's shoes and flower-sellers who sold posies to passers-by.

20 In the countryside, the craze for mechanization meant that machines were used to plough fields and carry out other farm duties. While this saved time, not everyone could afford these new advances in technology. For those farms that couldn't, many workers lost their jobs.

21 In 1846 the Corn Laws were abolished by Parliament. Originally brought in to protect farmers from cheap imported food, these laws raised food prices, causing great distress among the poor. When the Laws were removed, shoppers were delighted by the falling food bills, and this also created a bigger market for farmers to sell their produce.

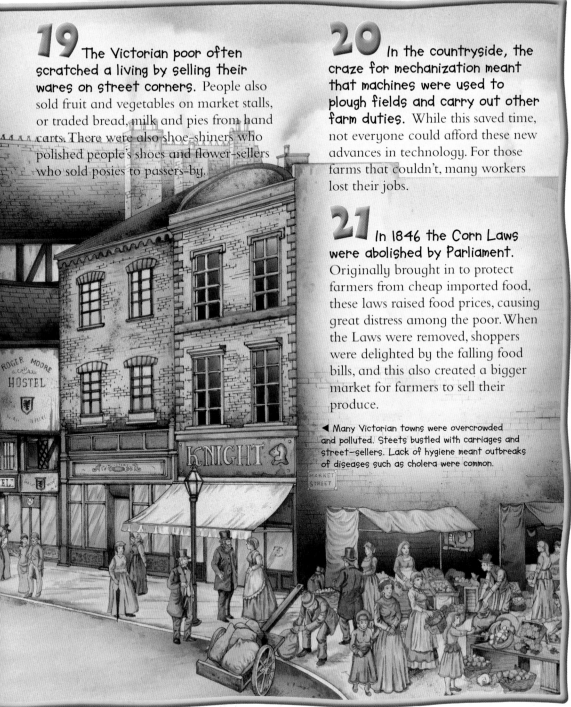

◄ Many Victorian towns were overcrowded and polluted. Steets bustled with carriages and street-sellers. Lack of hygiene meant outbreaks of diseases such as cholera were common.

Rich and poor

22 The poor lived in dirty, back-to-back terrace houses with just four rooms at best. They had no running water and one house was often home to a husband and wife and up to ten children. Brothers and sisters had to share rooms and privacy was non-existent.

▲ In Wales, Chartist protestors clashed with officials and many of the leaders of the movement were thrown into prison.

23 Homelessness was a growing problem in all the major cities. Those unable to work or too sick to enter the workhouse were thrown onto the streets. Many of the homeless were orphaned children. In 1867, Irishman Dr Thomas Barnado opened his first children's home in London to try and solve the problem.

▼ Poor couples often had as many as ten children – they often went hungry.

24 In the early years of Victoria's reign, Britain was in the grip of a depression. One group of people called the Chartists stirred up unrest by calling for the right to vote and demanding other reforms. Their fiery speeches caught the imagination of hungry audiences. Another movement, Marxism, proposed that everyone should be equal, all property should be owned by the State and that the monarchy should be abolished.

25 The poor of Ireland suffered a disaster in the 1840s when a potato blight (disease) destroyed their crops. Millions of tonnes of potatoes were ruined and many people died from diseases such as scurvy as they had no other food source to provide them with vitamins. Thousands of people died of starvation, while others fled abroad. It took the government a long time to realize just how bad the problem was.

I DON'T BELIEVE IT!

Rich Victorian women had to suffer to look good – they wore whalebone corsets strengthened with steel that must have been agony to wear.

26 For the rich, Victorian Britain was a wonderful place to live. They went to the theatre, the opera, flocked to musicals and attended lavish charity events. This high life was enjoyed not just by lords and ladies but by a new group of people who had become wealthy through the Industrial Revolution.

27 The rich devoted a lot of time and money to looking good and living well. Ladies wore fabulous dresses and expensive jewellery (often imported from India), and carried fans from the Far East. Men wore spats to protect their shoes from mud and tucked expensive walking sticks under their arms whenever they went out.

◀ Ballroom dancing was a popular way for the rich to spend their evenings.

Get a job!

28 **Factories and mills provided employment for the Victorian poor.** Men and women would work all day on dangerous, smelly machinery making goods to sell around the world. In small clothing factories called sweatshops, poor workers were hustled into cramped, dingy rooms to work from dawn to dusk earning barely enough money to survive.

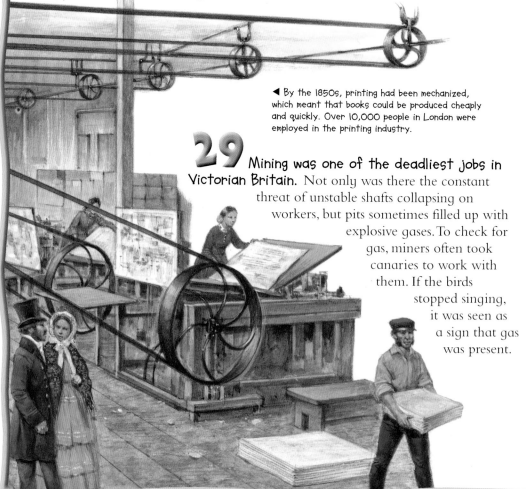

◀ By the 1850s, printing had been mechanized, which meant that books could be produced cheaply and quickly. Over 10,000 people in London were employed in the printing industry.

29 **Mining was one of the deadliest jobs in Victorian Britain.** Not only was there the constant threat of unstable shafts collapsing on workers, but pits sometimes filled up with explosive gases. To check for gas, miners often took canaries to work with them. If the birds stopped singing, it was seen as a sign that gas was present.

30 Going into service as a maid was the main career option for working-class girls. Work began at 6 a.m. and lasted until 10 p.m. Tasks ranged from stoking the fires and making the beds to serving meals and cleaning the house from top to bottom. Conditions for maids were harsh. They had no holidays, were forbidden from gossiping when on duty and often lived in freezing rooms without any form of heating, even in winter.

▶ Chimney sweep masters usually had child workers that they forced to climb up chimneys. Sometimes a fire was lit beneath the child to force them to climb higher.

31 Some people who struggled to find full-time jobs became pedlars. These poor people trundled from town to town trying to make a living from selling their wares. Their numbers included rag-gatherers, bone-pickers, cloth-sellers and animal skin traders. Some ended up in prison as they were driven to crime by desperate poverty.

◀ This woman is selling fruit. She would have worked long hours every day for very little money.

32 In poor families, everybody worked, including children. Small boys and girls as young as five were sent up sooty chimneys to sweep them clean, crawled down dark mines or wriggled under factory machines to unpick tangled threads. Many of these jobs were dangerous and thousands of children died every year at work. In 1842, the Mines Act was passed, banning children from working in mines.

JOB JUMBLE

Here are seven jobs jumbled up. Can you work out what they are?

1. diam 2. radlpe
3 michyen weeps
4. reachet 5. renmi
6. codrot 7. ghannam

Answers:
1. Maid 2. Pedlar
3. Chimney sweep 4. Teacher
5. Miner 6. Doctor
7. Hangman

Sent to the workhouse

33 The Poor Laws were made to encourage poor people to be less reliant on 'hand-outs'. This meant that to receive poor relief such as food or clothes, people had to live in the workhouse. The writer Charles Dickens (1812–1870) was so shocked by the conditions of workhouses that he wrote *Oliver Twist* to highlight the problem. He campaigned throughout his lifetime to turn public opinion against these terrible places.

▲ Charles Dickens wrote mainly about the problems of Victorian Britain, and in particular the desperate conditions of the poor.

▼ A scene from the 1968 musical *Oliver!*, based on Charles Dickens' novel *Oliver Twist*. The book tells the tale of a young orphan boy sent to a London workhouse.

34 Victorian authorities viewed poverty as a result of laziness, drunkenness and vice, and poor people were afraid of ending up in the workhouse. Inmates were separated from their families and were fed so little that many were literally starving. In one workhouse in Andover, Hampshire, people were seen scavenging for meat on the bones they were being forced to grind to make fertilizer.

▼ Food in the workhouse consisted mainly of a watery soup called gruel, and bread and cheese.

PUNISHMENT!

The scold's bridle was a particularly nasty punishment for badly behaved workhouse inmates. What did it stop the wearer doing?
a) Moving
b) Speaking
c) Eating
d) Crying

Answer:
b) it stopped the wearer from talking

35 Children without fathers were sent to the workhouse with their mothers if the family was too poor to support them. The Victorian public were shocked by such cruelty, however, and the law was changed to allow single mothers to make fathers pay towards the upkeep of their children.

36 The treatment in workhouses was harsh, and children were often beaten for misbehaving. At the Marylebone Workhouse in London, a scandal was caused by the number of children who ended up in hospital or even dead as a result of their terrible mistreatment.

Get me a doctor

37 **In 1867, English doctor Joseph Lister helped make surgery safer with the introduction of carbolic acid spray.** Lister realized that many deaths in hospital were caused by infection, and he invented a spray that could kill germs. Before this, many patients died from gangrene or infection soon after surgery, but the use of this spray meant deaths fell from 45 percent to 15 percent.

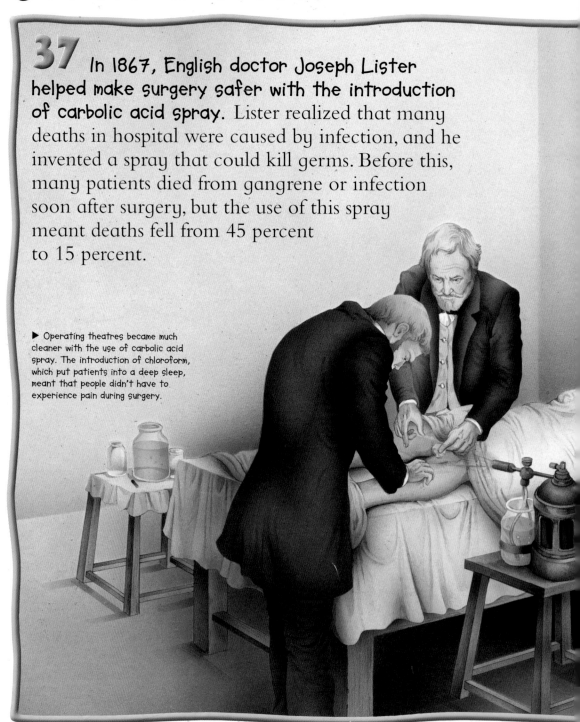

▶ Operating theatres became much cleaner with the use of carbolic acid spray. The introduction of chloroform, which put patients into a deep sleep, meant that people didn't have to experience pain during surgery.

38 Around 1850, the Scottish doctor Alexander Wood (1817–1884), invented the hypodermic syringe. The hollow, pointed needle (which could puncture the skin painlessly) was used to inject powerful painkilling drugs such as morphine and opium.

39 Victorian doctors made surgery less painful. For hundreds of years, patients had died on the operating table from shock. In 1847 an English doctor, John Snow, started using a chemical called chloroform that made people sleep during surgery. Queen Victoria's doctor, James Simpson, persuaded the queen to use the drug during the birth of Prince Leopold in 1853.

40 Doctors William Budd and John Snow prevented many Victorians dying from drinking dirty water. The two men realized that diseases such as cholera were carried in water, and they encouraged authorities to shut down infected pumps. The doctors' actions helped to dramatically reduce the number of deaths from water-borne diseases.

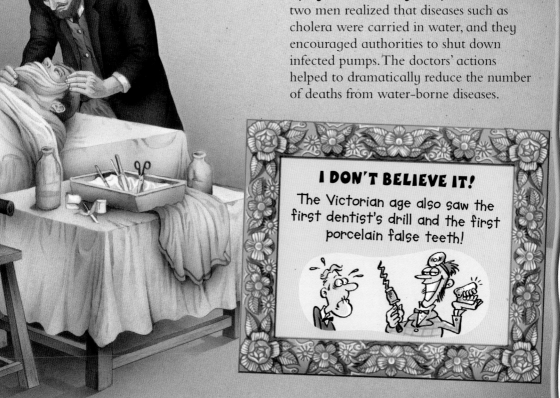

I DON'T BELIEVE IT!

The Victorian age also saw the first dentist's drill and the first porcelain false teeth!

Bright ideas

41 **During the reign of Queen Victoria, Britain was full of people with clever ideas.** Prince Albert was so impressed with the inventiveness of the Victorians that he held the Great Exhibition to show off their work. In 1851, over 14,000 men and women gathered in the newly built iron and glass Crystal Palace to show off their gadgets to millions of dazzled visitors.

42 **William Cook and Charles Wheatstone invented the Victorian Internet – the electric telegraph.** In 1837 the two Englishmen started to send messages down metal lines using electricity. In 1866, telegraph lines were laid under the Atlantic Ocean all the way to Canada using the first submarines.

▼ The Crystal Palace was a vast building, three times the length of St Paul's Cathedral and covered an area of 26 acres.

43 Joseph Swan brightened up Victorian houses in 1879 with the first working electric light bulb. By running electricity through a piece of wire called a filament inside a glass bulb, he was able to produce light. In 1883, Swan joined forces with the American Thomas Edison to create the Edison and Swan United Electric Lighting Company.

▼ Joseph Swan invented the lightbulb in 1860. The first filaments were made of paper coated in carbon.

▼ Victorians often looked stern and solemn in photographs because it took so long to expose the pictures – imagine having to pose a smile for up to one minute!

45 Vain Victorians were thrilled with the arrival of the first easy-to-use camera. In July 1857 Queen Victoria and her family posed for photographs using one of John Herschel and William Henry Fox Talbot's devices.

▶ As well as coming up with the idea of the telephone, Alexander Graham Bell also went on to invent the world's first method of recording sound, the gramophone.

44 Brilliant Scot Alexander Graham Bell came up with an invention that changed the world – the telephone. By transmitting speech electronically down wires, the telephone allowed people to talk to each other no matter where they were in the world. The first telephone call took place in 1876, when Bell rang his assistant and spoke the words, "Come here Watson, I want you." Bell's invention was so popular that by 1887 there were over 26,000 telephones in Britain.

Getting around

46 Victorian steam trains hurtled along their tracks. By 1900, 35,000 kilometres of track had been laid in Britain, while in 1863 the world's first underground station had opened in London as railways continued to develop at breakneck speed. One of the most famous routes ran from the West Country to London, and was designed by the engineer Isambard Kingdom Brunel (1806–1859). Passengers were so impressed that the Great Western Railway earned the nickname of 'God's Wonderful Railway'.

▲ Brunel was a great engineer who built ocean liners and bridges as well as railways.

58 Irishman Oscar Wilde was born in Dublin in 1854. In 1878 he moved to London to seek success as a writer and playwright. His most famous play was *The Importance of Being Earnest*, about the excesses of Victorian society. Wilde also wrote a novel, *The Picture of Dorian Gray*, and a collection of fairy tales.

60 Lewis Carroll (1832–1898) was the pen name of the Reverend Charles Lutwidge Dodgson. Although he never married, Carroll loved children, and wrote books including *Alice in Wonderland* and *Through the Looking Glass* for the daughters of friends. Carroll also wrote nonsense verse, including the poem 'Jabberwocky'.

▼ The Mad Hatter's tea party, where Alice takes tea with a collection of bizarre characters, is one of the most famous parts of Carroll's *Alice in Wonderland*.

59 In 1887, Irishman Bram Stoker (1847–1912) created one of the most terrifying horror stories ever written. *Dracula* is a tale about a vampire, based on east European legends, who lured victims to his castle in Transylvania to drink their blood so as to stay forever young. He had the power to transform himself into a bat, and could only be killed by driving a stake through his heart.

◀ *Dracula* has been made into dozens of films. This 1968 version starred Christopher Lee as Count Dracula.

ANAGRAM AGONY

Rearrange the sentences below to find the names of four famous books.

1. Wives tor lit
2. Any jeeer
3. Ada curl
4. In an odd wine cellar

Answers:
1. *Oliver Twist* 2. *Jane Eyre* 3. *Dracula* 4. *Alice in Wonderland*

Winding down

61 Thanks to the arrival of the new railways, holidays became readily available to the Victorian public. In 1841, Thomas Cook organized the first publicly advertised rail trip, carrying 570 excited passengers from Leicester to Loughborough. Cook eventually set up his own travel agency, which is still in business today. Educated young men and women travelled abroad on a 'Grand Tour' to places such as Switzerland, Paris and Italy, visiting sights such as Mount Vesuvius in Naples, Italy.

62 The Victorians loved trips to the seaside. Cheap rail travel meant that seaside resorts such as Blackpool in the north of England and Brighton on the south coast became popular holiday spots. Many people, including the royal family, enjoyed sea bathing, the wealthy often in bathing machines. These were horse-drawn huts that were wheeled into the sea, from where you could be lowered into the water by servants.

63 People in towns and cities enjoyed themselves by going to the theatre or music hall. Richer Victorians went to see the latest plays while the poor went to music halls, which were large rooms built at the side of pubs. There they could watch simple plays, or entertainers such as singers, dancers, jugglers and comics.

◀ Marie Lloyd was one of the most famous entertainers in Victorian Britain, and was given the nickname 'Queen of the Music Hall'. Her witty songs were loved by audiences.

◀ Rich and poor people flocked to the seaside during Queen Victoria's reign. It was thought the fresh air was good for your health.

64 The Victorians invented many of the world's most popular sports. Games such as football had been popular since the beginning of the century, but the Victorians introduced the first proper rules. In 1863, 11 teams met to form the first professional football league. Other popular games included tennis, bowls, croquet, cricket and rugby.

65 Wealthier Victorians wanting to escape England's dirty cities headed for Scotland. They were inspired by Queen Victoria and Prince Albert, who fell in love with the country and bought a home there called Balmoral Castle. In Scotland hunting, shooting and fishing became popular with royalty and the rich. So did watching the Highland Games, a competition of events that included tossing the caber (tree trunk) and shot putting.

I DON'T BELIEVE IT!

Funfairs first became popular in Victorian times, with a variety of steam-powered rides.

Build it!

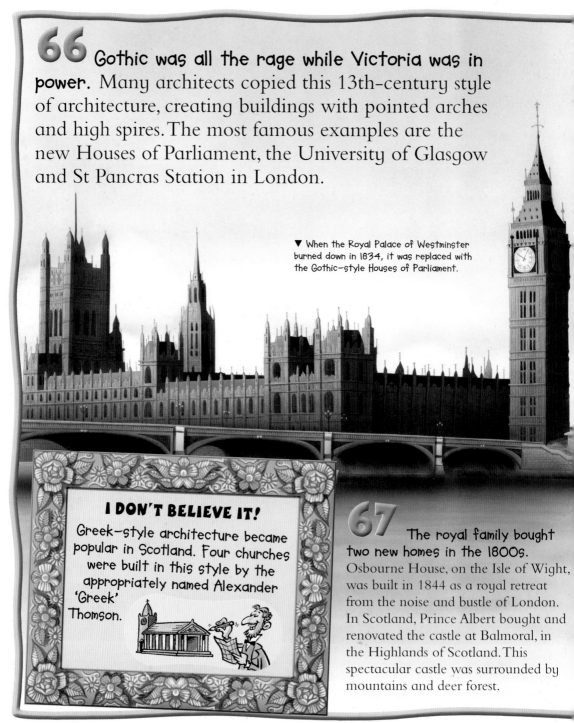

66 Gothic was all the rage while Victoria was in power. Many architects copied this 13th-century style of architecture, creating buildings with pointed arches and high spires. The most famous examples are the new Houses of Parliament, the University of Glasgow and St Pancras Station in London.

▼ When the Royal Palace of Westminster burned down in 1834, it was replaced with the Gothic-style Houses of Parliament.

I DON'T BELIEVE IT!

Greek-style architecture became popular in Scotland. Four churches were built in this style by the appropriately named Alexander 'Greek' Thomson.

67 The royal family bought two new homes in the 1800s. Osbourne House, on the Isle of Wight, was built in 1844 as a royal retreat from the noise and bustle of London. In Scotland, Prince Albert bought and renovated the castle at Balmoral, in the Highlands of Scotland. This spectacular castle was surrounded by mountains and deer forest.

68 **The Victorians loved to build with iron and glass.** Dramatic arched iron bridges strode across Britain's rivers, while at the Royal Botanic Gardens in Kew, an iron and glass frame protected the palm house from the harsh weather outside. Probably the most famous iron and glass building was the Crystal Palace, built to house the Great Exhibition in 1851. Sadly it burnt to the ground just a few years later.

69 **In Scotland, architect Charles Rennie Mackintosh was building great buildings out of stone blocks.** He designed the interior of the Willow Tea Rooms in Glasgow and filled it with mirrors and stencilled figures, created by his wife Margaret Macdonald. Mackintosh's best-known work was the Glasgow School of Art building, an imposing stone building that was begun in 1897.

▼ In 1890, the magnificent Forth Rail Bridge was opened, allowing trains to cross the Firth of Forth in Scotland. Designed by Sir John Fowler and Benjamin Parker, the bridge took seven years to complete.

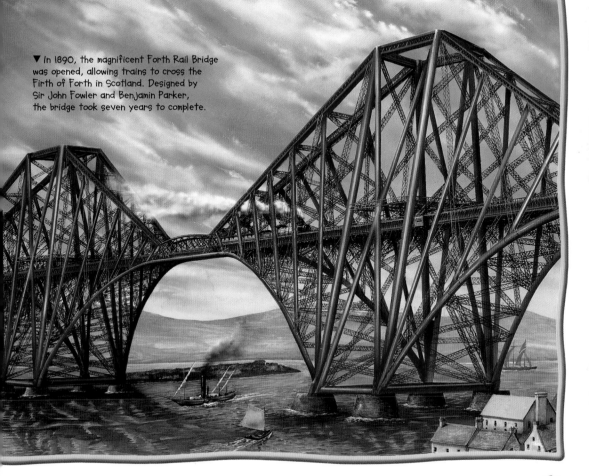

What's for dinner?

70 **Cooks in the 1800s had a problem keeping food fresh.** Meat or fish would go off after a few days, or even sooner in hot weather. To solve this problem, Victorian inventors built the first refrigerator in 1900. Food was chilled by cold air, circulated by a pump from ice blocks stored in a special compartment. Scientists also found a way to tin food, meaning that groceries such as fruit and vegetables could be kept fresh for months.

71 **Children throughout Victorian Britain were delighted by the arrival of ice–cream.** A famous cook called Agnes Marshall set up her own cookery school specializing in the delicious dessert. She claims to have made the first ice-cream cornet in 1888 and published a book called *Fancy Ices* in 1894.

▼ Victorian cooks worked extremely hard. All food was prepared by hand – from bread to soup and puddings.

72 Exotic foods brought back from the farthest corners of the Empire ended up on the dining tables of the wealthy. Fruits such as pineapples and kiwi became popular with the rich, while spices such as turmeric found their way into Victorian cooking pots. Tea, for a long time a luxury, became affordable for everybody.

Pineapple

Tea

▶ Pineapples were brought to Britain from the Caribbean, kiwi fruit from New Zealand and turmeric and tea from India.

Turmeric

Kiwi fruit

73 Fresh milk was delivered straight from the farm to the doors of Victorian houses. On set days, householders would carry out jugs to the passing milkman, who filled them from large churns. The ready availability of milk added Vitamin D to the diets of many malnourished children, helping to prevent diseases such as rickets.

▶ Victorian milkmen usually carried milk in large open pails hung from a wooden yoke across their shoulders.

74 Mrs Beeton became the world's first celebrity chef. The eldest girl among 17 children, she spent most of her childhood bringing up her younger brothers and sisters. She went on to find work as a magazine editor, and had the idea of collecting recipes sent in by readers to make into a book. In 1861, Mrs Beeton published *Mrs Beeton's Book of Household Management*, packed with recipes and tips for running a successful household.

MAKE ICE CREAM!

You will need:
large plastic bag ice 6 tbsp salt
1 tbsp sugar 1/2 pint milk
vanilla essence bowl
small plastic bag

1. Half fill the larger bag with ice, add the salt and seal it.

2. Mix the sugar with the milk and vanilla in a bowl, pour into the small bag and seal it.

3. Open the large bag, put the small bag inside and seal the large bag again.

4. Shake the bag for a few minutes. Your mixture will turn to ice cream!

Let us pray

75 Around 60 percent of Victorians regularly went to church on Sundays. New churches were built and old ones restored to cope with a religious revival. A bill to force people to attend church on Sundays was put forward in 1837, and Victorian society expected people to be hardworking and respectable.

▲ The Salvation Army helped the poor and needy. These London school children are enjoying breakfast supplied by army members in 1900.

76 English religious leader William Booth founded the Christian Mission in East London in 1865, which was renamed the Salvation Army in 1878. This army did not fight with bullets and swords but with the word of God. Booth organized members like an army to fight against sin and evil. The Salvation Army's aim was to show the love of God through Christianity and concern for the poorer classes.

◀ At the age of 13 William Booth was sent to work as an apprentice in a pawnbroker's shop. This experience helped him to understand the suffering endured by the Victorian poor.

77 **Many Victorians thought the Church of England was neglecting the poor.** The new Evangelical Church had a more caring attitude towards the less well-off and placed emphasis on helping the needy. It had also been responsible for pressing the government to abolish slavery throughout the Empire.

THE GALAPAGOS ISLANDS

▲ The remote Galapagos Islands are situated off the West coast of Ecuador. This map charts the route that Darwin took in his ship *The Beagle*.

78 **In 1859, Charles Darwin published *Origin of Species*, throwing religious leaders into a fury.** The book challenged the accepted idea that God created the world. In 1871, Darwin published *The Descent of Man*, which said that man evolved gradually from apes thousands of years ago. Darwin developed his ideas during a trip to the Galapagos Islands in South America, where he noticed that a single species of bird had evolved into many different kinds to adapt to different habitats.

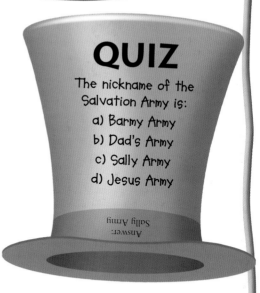

QUIZ

The nickname of the Salvation Army is:
a) Barmy Army
b) Dad's Army
c) Sally Army
d) Jesus Army

Answer:
Sally Army

79 **Religious beliefs were also challenged by the discovery of dinosaur fossils.** Finding fossils of creatures that lived millions of years before man was a shock, especially when the Bible said the world was created just a few thousand years ago. People found their religious faith being tested.

▼ The skull of the dinosaur *Heterodontosaurus*. Finding ancient fossil remains such as this made people question what was written in the Bible.

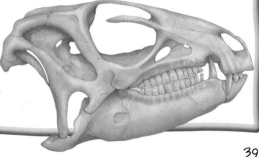

The long arm of the law

80 By 1856 most towns and cities had their own police force. The first police officers wore top hats and tailcoats, and wielded wooden truncheons. They were known as 'peelers' or 'bobbies' after Sir Robert Peel, who set up London's Metropolitan police force in 1829.

◀ Early policemen wore dark blue tailcoats with buttons up to the throat and reinforced top hats. This helped people recognize them easily.

81 To try to stop people committing crimes, the Victorians built lots of new prisons. Old gaols and rusting prison hulks (ships) could not cope with the crime rate, so between 1842 and 1877, 90 new lock-ups were built. Life inside was hard work and prisoners were not allowed to talk to each other. Many Victorians believed that this would make prisoners think about what they had done and face up to their responsibilities.

▲ Prisoners were made to exercise every day in the prison yard, by walking round and round in circles.

82 You could be locked up for not paying your debts in Victorian Britain. Houses of Correction such as Fleet, Clink, Bridewell and Marshalsea prisons in London held beggars, the homeless and those who owed money. They stayed behind bars until their debts were settled.

83 **Fewer people were sentenced to death in Victorian Britain than in the past.** Despite this, the hangman's noose remained the ultimate punishment. To make death more 'humane', authorities installed trap doors on the gallows, which helped break victims' necks more quickly when they dropped to their deaths.

▶ The sentence for a murderer was death by hanging.

84 **Pickpockets were a plague in large Victorian towns and cities.** Professional thieves, usually children, used their nimble fingers to lift items such as watches and jewellery from wealthy victims. Sometimes they followed men and women out of pubs, because drunken people made easier victims.

▼ Gangs of child pickpockets run by violent criminals were found in all the large cities in Britain.

85 **Science was helping to catch criminals for the first time.** In 1884 Sir Francis Dalton proposed the use of fingerprints to identify criminals, and soon after, detectives became able to spot the tiniest specks of blood on criminals' clothing. There were also methods for detecting the use of poisons, one of the most common forms of murder. Less successful ways to catch villains included physiology and the studying of prisoners' bodies to try to prove that they 'looked' different from ordinary people.

I DON'T BELIEVE IT!

People were so gripped by Sir Arthur Conan Doyle's stories about the fictional detective Sherlock Holmes that some were convinced he was a real policeman!

86 **The most famous villain in Victorian Britain was never caught by the police.** Jack the Ripper killed at least five women in East London in 1888. The killer also sent postcards to the police to taunt them, but he was never identified.

That'll teach them

87 In 1880, a new law stating that all children between the ages of five and ten must go to school, came into force. Because education was not free, however, few poor families could afford to send their children to school. In 1891, the law was changed again and schooling up to the age of 11 became free for all.

88 In 1818, a Portsmouth shoemaker called John Pounds started a free school for poor children. The idea was copied by others, and by 1852 there were over 200 of these 'ragged schools' in Britain. Conditions were often very basic. When Charles Dickens visited a ragged school in the 1840s he was said to be appalled by the state of the buildings and how dirty the children were.

▼ Victorian lessons concentrated on the 'three Rs' — Reading, wRiting and aRithmetic. Children learned by repeating lines until they were word perfect.

89

Many working–class children had to work all week, and had little chance to learn. Sunday (or Charity) schools were set up to try to give these children a basic education. Children were taught how to read and write, and attended Bible study classes.

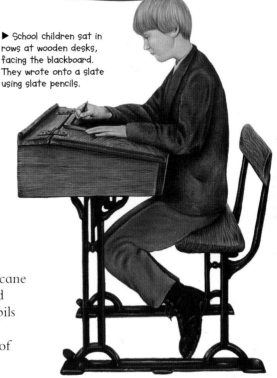

▶ School children sat in rows at wooden desks, facing the blackboard. They wrote onto a slate using slate pencils.

90

Naughty Victorian children faced punishments at school. Stern schoolmasters punished disobedient or disruptive children with the strap and the cane for 'crimes' such as leaving the playground without permission. Some teachers hit pupils so hard their canes snapped. To stop this happening, they stored their canes in jars of water to make them more supple!

I DON'T BELIEVE IT!

The most famous pickpocket is a character from *Oliver*. The Artful Dodger is a member of Fagin's gang, which gets Oliver into trouble.

▼ If children were particularly poor at a lesson such as maths, they would be made to sit in the corner wearing this dunce's hat! Sums were done using an abacus, a wooden frame with beads for counting.

Cane

Dunce's cap

Abacus

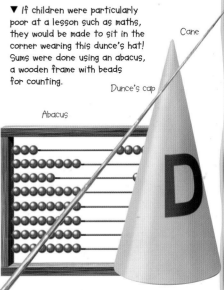

Family life

91 **For the Victorian middle class the home was the heart of family life.** It was a place to relax, have dinner, and somewhere to entertain friends. Working-class families preferred to spend leisure time elsewhere, as their homes were often dingy, smelly and cramped. They sometimes ate out, as cheap food was readily available from street stalls or pubs.

92 **Many Victorians played games to unwind in the evenings.** Battle lines were drawn over the ancient games of chess, backgammon and draughts, while darts was also popular. Children played games including blow football, Pin the Tail on the Donkey, Blind Man's Buff, Squeak Piggy Squeak and Snakes and Ladders.

▼ In the evenings, wealthy Victorian families gathered around a roaring fire to play games, listen to the piano or tell stories.

95 Naughty children were not tolerated by Victorian parents. If a child did something wrong he or she would be punished. Poor children often had to go to work, but richer children enjoyed a far more pampered lifestyle. They were looked after by nannies and nursemaids, and had expensive toys to play with. Rich children saw little of their parents, however, and were allowed an hour each evening to spend time with them before going to bed.

96 Victorians loved music. Many children and adults were able to play instruments. Sing-a-longs were extremely popular, with the whole family crowding round a piano to join in the fun. In 1887 the invention of the gramophone by Emile Berlinger in the USA made music more readily available for everyone.

▲ Toys such as this rocking horse would have been given to children by wealthy parents to help them get used to balancing on the back of a horse!

93 The Victorians had many Christmas customs that we still enjoy today. The idea of a white-bearded man called Father Christmas, who delivered gifts to children on Christmas Eve, was brought to Britain by Prince Albert. Victorians also introduced the practice of sending Christmas cards in 1846.

94 The Victorian father was strict and stern. He was obeyed by all the family and children were expected to call their father 'sir'. In rich households, fathers had a study, which the rest of the family were forbidden from entering without permission.

QUIZ

1. Which Victorian game, still played today, involved blindfolding an opponent?
2. Which Christmas tradition was introduced in 1846?
3. What was invented in 1887?

Answers:
1. Blind Man's Buff 2. Sending Christmas cards 3. The gramophone

End of an era

97 On 22 January 1901, Queen Victoria died, after more than 60 years on the throne. The Minister in Residence at Osbourne House, Arthur Balfour, broke the news at 6:40 p.m. *The Times* reported that 'all day long the Angel of Death has been hovering over Osbourne House... but at half-past six those wings were folded, and the Queen was at rest.'

▲ Queen Victoria's funeral cortege passes through the High Street, Windsor, on 2 February 1901. After lying in state, the queen was laid to rest at Frogmore Mausoleum on 4 February 1901.

98 After Victoria's death the throne passed to her son, Edward VII. Victoria had never trusted Edward, and had prevented him from interfering in important issues during her lifetime. When he became king, however, Edward devoted himself to his country, and became well-liked by the British public and across Europe.

◀ Kaiser Wilhelm II of Germany. Some people blamed the Kaiser for the start of World War I.

▲ Edward VII proved to be a good foreign ambassador for Britain as he was related to many of the European royal houses.

99 When he became king, Edward VII faced an immediate challenge from Germany. Led by Kaiser Wilhelm II, Victoria's grandson, the country began building its fleet of ships until it rivalled the Royal Navy in size. Four years after Edward died, the two countries were at war with each other.

100 King Edward VII tried to make life better for ordinary people. In 1902 he supported a new law making secondary education cheaper, and helped establish old age pensions in 1908. Despite this, the divide between rich and poor continued to grow, and it was not until the World War 1 in 1914 that people began to question their positions in society.

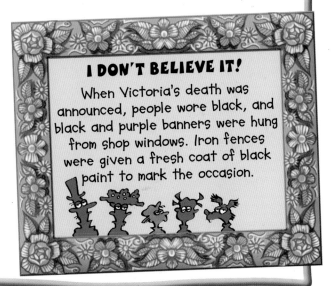

I DON'T BELIEVE IT!

When Victoria's death was announced, people wore black, and black and purple banners were hung from shop windows. Iron fences were given a fresh coat of black paint to mark the occasion.

Index